The Taste of Pomegranate Seeds

The Taste of Pomegranate Seeds

feel to heal / heal to feel

Sage Bava

RESOURCE *Publications* · Eugene, Oregon

THE TASTE OF POMEGRANATE SEEDS
feel to heal / heal to feel

Resource Publications
An Imprint of Wipf and Stock Publishers
199 W. 8th Ave., Suite 3
Eugene, OR 97401

www.wipfandstock.com

PAPERBACK ISBN: 979-8-3852-4659-5
HARDCOVER ISBN: 979-8-3852-4660-1
EBOOK ISBN: 979-8-3852-4661-8

04/23/25

To my mother and sister, whose love and grit inspire me; to everyone who nurtures safe spaces; and to you, who found these pages on your journey.

Contents

CONTENTS

II. LEARNING
IN THE DARK

CONTENTS

Preface

Derealization and depersonalization—these are names for what happens when the mind fractures under the weight of experience. They are common after trauma, after loss, after hardship. To name them is to strip them of their power. To understand them is to know they are not permanent, only a passage, not a destination.

This poetry book began as my own healing journey from years of struggling with dissociation—of looking in the mirror and not recognizing who was there, of feeling like a ghost in my own body. Reality felt distant, as if I were slipping through the cracks of existence. But the end of the tunnel came, and when it did, the light was sweeter for the darkness that had come before it.

Pomegranate seeds hold a taste that lingers—sweetness entwined with sharp bitterness, a reminder that joy and sorrow are never far apart. In Greek mythology, Persephone's story is a testament to this paradox. Abducted by Hades and drawn into the underworld, she is forever changed, her fate sealed by the pomegranate's crimson seeds. In consuming them, she binds herself to shadow, yet in doing so, she also claims her own power. No longer merely a daughter of spring, she becomes the queen of both realms—of darkness and light, descent and return, death, and renewal. Hers is not just a myth of captivity but of seasons—both those that shape the earth and those that shape the soul. With her descent, winter arrives—a time of stillness, loss, and surrender. Yet spring always follows, as she rises once more, bringing renewal. This eternal rhythm belongs not only to nature but to us as well.

We, too, must endure winters of grief, sit in the silence of what has been lost, and trust in the promise of bloom.

I know what it means to be lost between worlds. The feeling of being "unreal" is terrifying. Floating outside oneself, watching from a distance, feeling untethered. For years, I didn't have the language for it. I only knew I was drifting, that time had become something I observed rather than lived. This book is for anyone who has ever felt that way. For those caught in the vortex of dissociation, uncertain of what is happening. I am not a therapist—I do music mostly—but I know what it means to search for something that reflects your inner world, to find words that make you feel less alone.

You are not going insane. Or perhaps you are, just a little—but that's okay. You'll come back. The soul has a way of finding home. For me, it was a spiritual journey that led me back into my body— a slow return from the clouds, a breath, a reconnection. I began to understand that there are two worlds: the vast, infinite truth of the universe and the fragile construct of man's reality. Sometimes, souls get lost in the construct. We forget the rhythm beneath the noise. But we are never truly lost. We only need to remember, to feel, to let ourselves become unstuck.

This collection is a series of photographs from my life, each poem a snapshot of a moment that shaped me—pieces of grief, love, healing, and surrender. It was born from the desire to share and connect, to offer proof that no pain lasts forever, that even the most brutal winters eventually give way to spring. These poems do not seek to provide answers; rather, they invite you to sit with your grief, to breathe into your healing, and to recognize the beauty in transformation.

My hope is that these words bring solace, a reminder that you are never truly alone. Whether you stand in heartbreak, at the edge of change, or in quiet reflection, may these poems offer companionship—a lantern in the dark, a breath of spring after the longest winter.

Like Persephone, may you embrace the wholeness of life— the sweetness and the bitterness, the descent, and the ascent. May you walk boldly through your seasons, knowing that every ending carries the seed of beginning, and that even in the deepest dark, the pomegranate still ripens, waiting to be tasted.

Getting unstuck. You are love. You are loved. You are the universe.

"And Persephone, full of wisdom, spoke to her mother: 'Mother, I have returned, but the underworld's shadow lingers in my heart. Yet in this, too, there is balance—for I have seen what lies below and what lies above, and I will walk between them forever."

(Homeric Hymn to Demeter, lines 410–420, paraphrased from the original theme)

I. DEREALIZATION
in the cloud

A STOIC DANCE

kick in the gut
awakens me
morning after morning
days blend, nights disappear
a sad stoic dance with dissociation
an addict to this numbness
no matter where I go
where I hide
wrapping myself
around the
flesh of
you

SPECTER OF THE SELF

Derealization: the world feels unreal—a fog where walls bend and breathe, voices drift like smoke, and my hand passes through. I cannot tell if I am here, or just a shadow in someone else's dream.

Depersonalization: Identity shattered under my skin, each fragment a stranger's reflection, split between glass and breath, between what happened and the story my mind keeps telling.

He is gone, but his shadow lingers—
a stain on the floor, a whisper in the walls,
following me, close as my pulse, distant as the stars.

I cannot sit in rooms
the walls close in like a breath held too long, each second stretching into an eternity of absence, a void that echoes with nothingness. The air thickens with an invisible weight— a presence of what is missing, the ghost of my own company.

It is as if the space itself recoils
from my being,
as if the silence grows heavier
with the sound of my unspoken thoughts.

To be alone is to be with the emptiness,
an entity that shadows me
like an unwelcome guest.
I look into the corners,
expecting to see someone—

maybe 'self'. . .
she is no longer there.

Yet to be with others is another kind of exile,
a different solitude wrapped in noise and skin.
Their words bounce off me,
like raindrops off glass—
heard, but never felt.
I smile, I nod,
I mimic the rhythms of belonging,
but inside, I am a chasm,
a hollow that cannot be filled,
a body with no weight,
a voice with no echo.

Who am I to be in this strange existence?
A ghost in a room of shadows?
Something lesser,
a half-formed thought,
a flicker on the edge of vision?

Wondering if I'm meant to inhabit
this in-between, this liminal space
where I'm neither seen nor unseen,
known nor unknown—
just a breath in the wind,
a whisper in an empty hall,
a specter seeking substance
in a world that seems
to pass through me
like light through mist.

SILENCE: A GENISIS

I commune with silence now,
not as an adversary to vanquish,
but as an ancient confidant, somber and clandestine,
one who discerns the tessellations of my despair,
who measures the gravity of my desolation
pressed into the marrow of my being,
and holds it with an unspoken tenderness,
an embrace that asks for nothing in return.

Silence arrives like an enigmatic guest,
draped in shadows woven from twilight's skeins,
its presence, a gossamer cloak settling over me,
heavy with the dust of forgotten moments.
It breathes stories that dwell beneath the surface—
underneath the city's murmur—
the low rumble of unseen engines,
the susurration of wind through leafless branches,
the delicate crackle of thoughts splitting open
like seeds in the dark loam of my mind.

Within this profound quietude, I discern truths
that language has failed to articulate—
the cadenced thrum of my pulse,
a resolute metronome,
marking time against the chasm of emptiness,
the heartbeat, a whisper in the cathedral of my chest,
a prayer, soft and tremulous,
uttered into the abyss.

It is the silence that enfolds me,
like a vast, unseen constellation,
its arms stretching wide across the firmament of my fractured spirit,
reminding me with each slow, rhythmic pulse, that I endure, that
I persist—
inhabiting this fragile, ephemeral vessel
even as the cosmos contracts around me.

In this sanctuary of stillness,
I unearth a peculiar tranquility—
a solace that does not seek absolution,
that thrives in the interstices of breath,
where my body begins to anchor,
finding gravity in the earth's deliberate spin.
And in this reverent silence,
I dare to believe that I am sufficient,
that this, too, can be a genesis,
a place from which to unfurl anew

ONCE SO HUMAN

I knew why I was trapped here,
Longing to strip away the last traces of this mortal guise,
Seeking to escape the weight of flesh,
    Desiring release from the bonds of human frailty.

Longing to be a machine,
a seamless construct of steel and sinew,
where the hum of gears
drowns out the cacophony of feeling.
To exist not in the realm of emotions,
but in the stark efficiency of operation,
to be an entity of cogs and unnamable materials,
where each turn, each movement,
is a calculated precision.

Fill me with mechanisms
that tick in measured time,
with circuits that pulse with purpose,
not emotion.
Let me be crafted from alloys
that absorb stress without complaint,
from substances that withstand
the wear of existence without lament.

I yearn for the clarity of function,
where purpose is defined by performance,
where the intricacies of my being
are encoded in the language of machinery.

To feel the steady rhythm of my internal clock,
the predictable dance of my pistons,
the cold assurance of metal
that neither fears nor desires.

In this form,
I would be free from the soul,
unburdened by the flux of feeling,
a synthesis of parts that serve
a single, unwavering function.
No more the ambiguity of human experience,
but a harmonious symphony
of engineered intent,
where I am defined by my mechanics,
and my purpose is clear and unclouded.

WORDS TO EXPLAIN

derealization. . .
continuum of moments that aren't there
memories that happened but weren't lived
pulling the plug, not feeling or thinking

depersonalization. . .
uninhabited heads
riding upon bodies whose only signs of life
are the stirring jolting pains of remembrance
before the echoes of ghosts have been sedated
so one may look down from above and see it all play out

19

Nineteen, traversing the sprawling veins of New York City,
a labyrinthine expanse
where the skyline cleaves the heavens
and every street corner whispers promises
that dissolve into the haze of my disorientation.

The city pulses with a frenetic cadence,
a heartbeat I struggle to synchronize with,
each subway jolt a stark reminder
of my detachment,
adrift in this urban mosaic
like a specter amidst the cold, unfeeling architecture.

Derealization enshrouds me in a translucent veil,
distorting the known into an alien tapestry.
The sidewalks dissolve into smudged watercolor strokes,
faces morph into faceless masks,
their expressions vacuous,
eluding my grasp.
I reach out into the void,
but am tethered to an ephemeral nothingness,
adrift in a realm that resists anchoring.

Amid this urban maelstrom,
Seeking vestiges of the sacred,
a glimmer of spirituality
to thread through the dissonant edges of my reality.

I find fleeting solace in the hush of ancient churches,
their stained, glass windows refracting a kaleidoscope of distant divinity,
a shimmering hint of transcendence
amidst the cacophony of steel and stone.

In the verdant embrace of Central Park,
where the trees stand as solemn guardians,
their roots delving deep into the earth's ancient embrace,
I find a semblance of enduring reality.
I close my eyes and strain to hear the divine murmur,
but the city's relentless clamor
drowns out the fragile cries of my spirit.

MIRAGE

And the scariest part?
I didn't know its name—
this elusive specter that had taken root,
a silent usurper of my very essence.
It wove itself into me,
a shadow that obscured every corner of my mind,
leaving me adrift in an unknown sea.

This thing, this nameless force,
had invaded my thoughts,
erasing the markers of who I once was.
Memories, once vivid and anchored,
now dissolved into a fog of forgetfulness,
each recollection slipping through my fingers
like sand in a windstorm.

I could no longer grasp the contours of my past,
the deeds and decisions that had shaped me,
now obscured by a veil of confusion.
What had I done? The question echoed,
unanswered and haunting,
lost in the void created by this presence.

It was only now
but now was a mirage,
a fleeting moment that seemed to evaporate
before it could be fully grasped.

The present, though palpable,
felt like a hollow echo,
a reflection that did not quite align
with the reality I once knew.

I was not here
in the way I used to be,
not present in the moment,
but a specter, a ghost wandering
through the remnants of a life now altered.
The sense of self that once anchored me
was replaced by an emptiness
that stretched infinitely,
a gaping chasm where identity once resided.

And so I drifted,
caught in the throes of this nameless dread,
a prisoner of my own mind's disarray.
The scariest part of all
was not just the disorientation,
but the haunting realization
that I was lost in a landscape
where the self-had been swallowed
by an unnamable force,
and I was left to wander
in the echoing silence
of my own forgotten existence.

NIGHT 1,096

Ask the moon,
how it feels to be isolated in darkness?
in this city. . .where the pollution blocks out all the stars
she says the light is inside her, so she needs for nothing.
envy her,
but be glad she is there.

SCORNED BIRDS

Rumination

cacophony of familiar voices deafeningly echoing
in all corners of my mind
laying on the cold floor of my unconscious curled up
as small as possible.

but it still finds me.

the cyclical thought patterns taking
turns diving down like scorned
birds taking their revenge.

SOLACE

I only felt solace in the eyes of those who looked upon me as he did—
something to possess, to gaze upon with a predatory longing.
In those eyes, I saw a reflection of myself,
a mere outline of flesh and desire,
a ripe body framed by the shadows of a deeper need.
They looked right through me,
past the surface of my being,
to the fractured soul beneath
screaming for salvation with a numb mouth
and a throat choked by unspoken cries.

I only felt solace with him
who was twice my age and half my heart,
his sharp eyes piercing through the veneer of pretense,
seeing me not as a person but as an object
to be possessed, to be consumed.
His eyes held a cold, dispassionate clarity,
a mirror to my own fractured self,
where solace was found in the illusion of connection,
but never in the reality of mutual understanding.

I only felt solace in rooms
where the space was devoid of soul,
where the air was thick with the weight of unspoken truths
and the absence of real reckoning.
In these empty chambers,
where reality was stripped away,
I found a perverse comfort,

a fleeting escape from the introspection
that lay beyond the cold, clinical gaze.

I only felt solace in rooms
where the essence of being was as thin as the walls that enclosed me,
I could momentarily forget the depth of my own emptiness,
the void that echoed with every hollow word
and every unfulfilled promise.
Here, amidst the absence of genuine engagement,
I found a fleeting peace,
a solace born not of true connection,
but of the quiet surrender to the roles
we played in each other's empty lives.

So I drifted through these moments,
seeking solace in the gaze of those who saw only my surface,
and in the rooms where the soul was an afterthought,
a place to be touched but never truly known.
In these shadows, I found a fleeting comfort,
a temporary balm for a heart that yearned for something real,
even as it remained locked in a world
where true solace was always just beyond reach.

BOOMERNG

in the light, think of the past in the
night, dream of it
stuck.

fck.

WAR

I thought we settled the score,
but you kept digging for more—
throwing punches and slamming doors.

The voice in my head tells me to drop,
saying I'll never be good enough,
keeps me up all night,
finding satisfaction in our fights.

We have to work together, head and heart,
to get better;
you kept coming for more.
You fed off all the darkness,
so I kept trying to let the light in,
hoping to win the war.

Are you the voice in my head?
All the way back from the dead?
Telling me all that was left unsaid,
it should have been me instead?

Is it you?
The shadow clinging to my thoughts,
the echo reverberating through my mind—
a presence insisting on being heard,
an unwelcome reminder of past hurts
and unhealed wounds?

The struggle is not just against your memory,
but against the parts of me that still resonate with your influence.
I grapple with the remnants of what was shared,
the intense emotions lingering in quiet moments of reflection.

The challenge lies in distinguishing
between what is mine and what was left behind.
Untangling the threads of our history
from the fabric of my present self
is an ongoing battle—
to reclaim my sense of self from the shadows
of what once was.

Facing these echoes,
their weight unfolds,
a path emerges—
existence reshaped,
beyond the lingering shadow.

WHO SHOULD I BE?

. . .and there it is again
       craving that feeling. . .
             chaos. . . .
                     the danger
                           the darkness
                       evoked in eyes that linger. . .

. . .can i pretend to be another. . .again. . .
to claim an identity that can look at and withstand evil. . .
                    who should i be tonight?

CLOUDY, WITH A CHANCE OF BEING OUT OF MY BODY

Each day I wonder who I will be when I wake
Never myself, always some archetype
A perceived play
Cloudy, with a chance of being out of my body
Looking down from above
Cloudy, with a chance of slipping from flesh,
Each day a grotesque unveiling—who will emerge from the inward fog?
Morphing through forms in a macabre masquerade.

Each dawn, a new mask draped over a rotting frame,
An endless cycle of faceless disguises,
Bound not by identity but by the roles I assume,
Wandering through a nightmare of ever-shifting selves.

Were the clouds there to protect or to harm?

Shielding me from visions inside but keeping me from being alive

OF THAT I'M SURE

I think you might
be an angel,
with lips so warm,
eyes that burn,
silky skin that makes me yearn
to quiver with you,
wet and warm,
every time I am reborn.

You taste like heaven,
but it feels like hell—
the tug of war
between wanting and needing,
unhealthy love

I think you might
be the devil,
fill my head and heart with dread.
Every time I lay in bed,
waking up alone,
biting my nails,
so far from home.

The echoes of your touch
linger like a phantom,
pulling me back to the edge
of a precipice I cannot escape.
Far from home,

adrift in the aftermath
of our fractured devotion,
I am left to navigate
the wreckage of my longing,
caught between the heaven
you offered
and the hell that followed.

In the quiet spaces of the night,
I grapple with the remnants
of our intoxicated encounters,
haunted by a love that is both divine
and devastatingly cruel.
And though I seek solace
in the cold light of day,
I am forever ensnared
by the echoes of what we were,
torn between the ecstasy
and the agony
you left behind

SUBMISSION

something 'bout giving up control
something 'bout playing a role
i want to give it all to you
tell me what you want me to do
until we become

        one

tell me what you want me to do
i want to please you
i want to tell you what to do

kiss me all over
elbows and shoulders
until we become

        one

STRANGE MEN

the lipstick that was bled
pillows on the beds
after all those lies he said
wrinkled eyes
stained with icy greed
can't hear silent screams
eyeliner hides the baby
beautiful she's so beautiful such an old soul
shines through her darkening exterior
17 living in her dreams
younger than she seems
making bizarre realities

WHEN YOU USE THE SOUL

The body will follow.

Descending into a festering abyss,
where light rots away and shadows writhe.
It starts as a gnawing itch, a seeping rot,
a spiritual cancer that erupts into flesh.

The mind, once a vibrant expanse,
turns into a putrid wasteland,
where dread crystallizes into visceral torment,
and each breath is a rasping gasp,
a slow suffocation in a mire of decay.

In the silence, the soul's hunger festers—
an insatiable maw that devours from within,
turning vitality into a relic.
The pulse falters,
a shuddering beat of a forgotten heart.

In the cracked mirror, you confront the truth
carved into lifeless skin,
a map of the internal malaise
revealing itself in every convulsion,
every tremor of a body lost.

And as you stumble through the charnel house
of a diminished existence,
you yearn for a glimpse of redemption,
a return to a semblance of wholeness
that now seems as distant
as the farthest reaches of despair.

For when you neglect the soul,
the body inevitably follows,
an echo of the spirit's plea,
a reminder of the fragile tether
between the heart's agony
and the body's lifeline.

UNWELL

i was hollow
the pits on my face
defined me
small fires
needing water
    a perished sense of self
erupting under the skin
dark energies
engulfing every crevice
microbiome senses this
    immune compromised sick
             skin burns and flakes
               -internal erosion

YOU TASTE SWEET

baptize me in your juices.

NATURE

I dream of drinking from them
like an ancient chalice of soul,
letting their essence spill into me,
a wine that stains
everything it touches.

I want to feel it pour down my throat,
past my heart, my ribs, my belly button,
warming the deepest hollows of my being,
until it reaches that buried place
where want becomes need,
where hunger finds its voice
in a cry of ecstasy we share,
a sound that splits the air
with something raw,
something that feels like truth.

But I know I cannot have this—
not yet, not with this body I have sold
to half-truths and empty promises,
to hands that never cared
to learn my secret language.
This soul, too—
I did not know when I sold it,
but now I see the cost.
The weight of it bears down,
like an iron shackle wrapped around
what's left of my tenderness.

I wish to be cleansed,
to be worthy of her touch,
to press my lips to her pulse
and feel something holy
stirring in the marrow of my bones.
But there is a price for every betrayal,
a reckoning in every embrace.

I dream of her lips, still—
of how they might taste like forgiveness,
like an answer to a question
I've been too afraid to ask myself.
But what can I give her
when my own reflection
feels like a stranger's face?
What can I offer,
when all I have is this emptiness
and the echo of what I used
to be?

I want to learn her,
to savor the salt and sweetness
of her skin,
to trace her spine like a pilgrim
on a sacred path.
But the map is smudged
with old wounds,
and my hands tremble
with guilt.

So, I stand at the edge of wanting,
knowing that desire is not enough
when the soul is in arrears.
I long for her touch to awaken me,
but until I reclaim what I have lost,
until I stitch myself whole again,
I cannot drink from her lips,
cannot taste that communion.

I am left to wander this desert
of my own making,
thirsty for her love
and the love I must find within,
before I can ever be worthy
of that sacred, ancient chalice
that her lips offer to mine.

do i love her or am i just traumatized by men?

NO VOICE

I can't seem to find the words
that don't hurt when they come out.
My throat closes every time
the truth rears its head.
Perhaps my body thinks
that staying silent
is the best survival method.

22

The year where harmony is called upon—
and if it dares break from the heavens
to strike the earth and reach the depths of hell
where it is needed, it will.

This was the year of remember,
the year the stars shifted in their cold orbits,
casting their indifferent light
on a mind newly awakened.
The year I found more autonomy—
in my mind, my body, my desire, myself.

Still, I am a small inhabitant in my large body,
roaming this vast and unpredictable earth
with feet that ache from the journey,
but there is a twinkle of hope, a gleam,
like a hidden spring in the heart of a desert
long unyielding, unforgiving, unchanged.
I remembered.

The taste of freedom, sharp on my tongue,
like citrus bitten into after a long fast,
my senses alive, the air electric
with all I could become.
I began to listen to the songs
my body whispered to itself in the dark,
ancient melodies of knowing
that I had buried beneath layers of doubt and fear.

At 22, I learned to read the braille of my own skin,
the stories etched deep by hands
that never understood my shape.
I reclaimed the narrative—
stitched the jagged seams together
with threads of something like self-love,
but more tender, more fierce,
a self-compassion that doesn't flinch
from the mirror or the memory.

This was the year I stopped shrinking
to fit the spaces I was given.
I expanded. I unfurled.
in my own shadow and breathed deep,
letting my lungs fill with all the air
I had been denied.
22. The year I stopped apologizing
for the hunger in my heart,
the fire in my belly,
the wild in my spirit.

Still, I wander—
a soul in a body that is still learning
its boundaries, its limits, its power.
But now, there is a map,
not etched in stone or ink,
but in the pulse of my veins,
in the rhythm of my breath.

I am guided by the stars
that once seemed so distant,
now a little closer,
a little more aligned with the path I forge.

This is the year where harmony is more than a wish,
more than a distant celestial balance.
It is something I call down from the heavens
to reside in my bones, to walk with me,
to break bread with me at the table of my becoming.
A harmony that strikes the earth
and ripples through my core,
grounding me in the present
while whispering of all that is still possible.

The year I learned that the desert
does not have the final say,
that water can be drawn from stone,
and that even in the driest seasons,
something green and sacred
can break through the cracked earth
and reach for the sun.

II. LEARNING
In the dark

perhaps the lessons we must learn are presented

viscerally

to walk through the dark and the cloud and the light

IT ARRIVED WITHOUT WARNING—

like a storm splitting the clear blue sky,
an uninvited guest in the sanctuary of my mind.
The air shifted, grew thick,
and suddenly, I was elsewhere,
not here in this room, but there,
where time folds in on itself
and everything sharpens—
sounds, sights, the weight of breathing.

It started as a tremor
beneath the surface, a quickening pulse,
the heat of my skin turning cold,
the familiar world shifting
into something jagged and unreal.
A flash—
and then I am trapped inside it,
the past flooding back with a vengeance,
a memory that is not memory,
but something more alive,
something that bites and claws.

The walls of the room close in,
or maybe they stretch endlessly—
I can't tell.
The air is too thick to draw in,
my lungs are clenched fists.
Every sound is too loud—
the rustle of paper, the hum of a distant car,

the sound of my own blood
pounding in my ears like war drums.
I try to remind myself
where I am, who I am,
but my body has forgotten—
it only knows the fear, the panic,
the relentless replay of what once was.

I see faces that aren't there,
hear voices that have long since faded.
I am split between now and then,
torn by the tension of two realities colliding,
my hands shaking as they reach
for something real, something solid
to anchor me back to the present.
But nothing is solid—
not even my own bones.

I know it's a trick of the mind,
a cruel, looping game my neurons play,
but knowing does nothing
to ease the grip of it—
the way my body betrays me,
goes rigid, then limp,
like a marionette's strings cut loose.
I want to run, I want to scream,
but I am frozen, a statue carved
from the cold stone of fear.

It feels like forever before I surface—
before the world starts to make sense again,
before I can breathe without tasting smoke,
before I remember this is now
and not then.

I feel a strange exhaustion,
a weariness that seeps into my bones,
and I wonder how something
that happened so long ago
can still feel like it's happening right now—
how the past can haunt the body
like a restless ghost,
how it can take up residence
in the mind, in the muscles,
in the marrow of being.

And I know this isn't the end—
just the beginning of a battle
I hadn't known I was still fighting.

IF ONLY I KNEW

the wall throbbed
        with faint heartbeats that
quickened as if operating in fight or
flight
        an evil had entered
        too cunning to notice
        the trauma spread. . .
            invading each material
        and then
                our flesh

        on the day it took
        ahold of my brain
        shadows filled
        every crevice

        just slow enough to not be alarmed
        an anaconda hug that made me warm and
numb

        until it squeezed too much to handle for a little skinny
girl the pain was visceral but not my own how does one carry
around this heavy snake?

not possible
i saw her crumbling, fighting every day
demons residing and feeding
if only i knew

PANDORA'S BOX

Although her story was not mine
It was the start

        and so, the box was open, and evil played.

A PLANNED PROGRESSION

       . . . . .first he was a
        watchful eye then his father
therapist
        producer
friend
        teacher
self-proclaimed soul mate
            stop

                stop

                    s

                to

                p

                    s

            top
        the voice
    inside me yelled
        but nothing
        came out

a progression i didn't know he had planned from the start

KIDNAPPED

Run fast
from the rule book, whiplash from that first look—
age is but a number,
I heard through their slumber.
I was just a baby
when you came and took my heart,
stole the parts,
you were a work of art.

Stole my innocence,
used my ignorance—
I didn't see any other way.
Take me away,
pull me under your waves,
deep into your shadowed tide,
where it's easier to lay underwater than gasp in open air.

Kidnapped—
fingers capture the words from my mouth,
kiss me into the shroud of your spell
where there was nothing to tell,
just the weight of your hand,
and the burn of your gaze
that made me believe I was more than I was,
that made me want to be less than myself.

Take me,
and the child I used to be,

fold her into your story.
Now it all seems so long ago,
the way she broke in your hands,
the way she bent to your will,
how she dissolved like sugar on the tip of your tongue.

And still, she longs for the moment
before she knew what she knows now—
before the bruises bloomed beneath her skin,
before the ache settled into her bones.

She wishes she could run fast enough
to shed the parts you gave,
to shake off the spell you cast,
but the road stretches on,
and she is still learning how to walk it alone.

ANTIDOTE

The allowing hurt more than the doing.
Dissociation—my most trusted ally.

I became the story,
a fading thread,
unraveling in silence.

But silence does not erase,
it only waits.

PERSEPHONE IN THE FEILD

The sun licked her shoulders like a golden serpent, draping her in a haze of drowsy freedom. Fingers, soil-tinged and soft, plucked blooms with careless grace, violets and narcissus cradled like newborns. Her laughter tangled in the air, a thread of innocence in the wild loom of spring. The grass whispered secrets beneath her feet—warnings lost to the hum of her delight. The ground sighed, split, and bled shadow. She gasped, not from fear, but the thrill of a world upending itself at her feet, unveiling a depth she didn't know. Before she could speak, the dark reached up, its tendrils coiling around her ankles, its whispers slick with hunger. It stole her breath, her blossoms, her name— dragging her from light's sweet blindness to the fathomless undercurrent of her own becoming.

The Descent—(*Swallowed Whole*)

She sank, fighting the jaws of the earth, her curiosity sharpening as roots brushed her skin—fingers weaving a net, not to hold, but to guide. The underworld opened like a wound, its breath damp with decay and longing. Here, the air had teeth, biting her cheeks with shadows, tonguing the pulse in her throat. The one who waited—a king, not of men, but of hunger— offered his hand like a serpent offering its skin. "Eat," he murmured, voice thick with velvet and ash, his smile a cracked crescent of bone. The seeds were slick, red, like the blood of her own curiosity. She swallowed—each bite an iron thread stitching her to this place, this darkness that both repelled and remade her.

Queen of Both Worlds—(*The Return of Shadow*)

She emerged, a daughter of daylight, her innocence draped like a veil over a face that had tasted the tongue of shadows. The flowers she once gathered wilted in her hands, unfit for the queen she had become. Her eyes held a serpent's gleam, the knowing that cuts and coils at once. She walked among mortals, each step rooted in the weight of the underworld, her laughter brittle, sharp as the edge of a broken mirror. No longer merely light, no longer merely dark, she was a thread pulled taut between. Her mother wept for her daughter's stolen days, but Persephone could not, her lips still stained with the taste of pomegranate.

For she had learned what no meadow could teach: that the dark does not take without giving, that even the wildest winds must bow to the quiet weight of the earth, that innocence is not lost— it is transformed.

POMEGRANATE SEEDS

1 in 5 women know the taste—
pomegranate seeds,
bitter and bursting
with silent rage.
No questions.
No permission.
Just a hand that pulled,
a body that said, *be still.*
Their breath replaced by his.
Their light swallowed whole.
Hades offered seeds,
a contract disguised as sweetness.
They ate, not knowing
their roots would anchor in his shadow.
But peace lilies bloom in darkness,
and even stolen souls
can be found again.

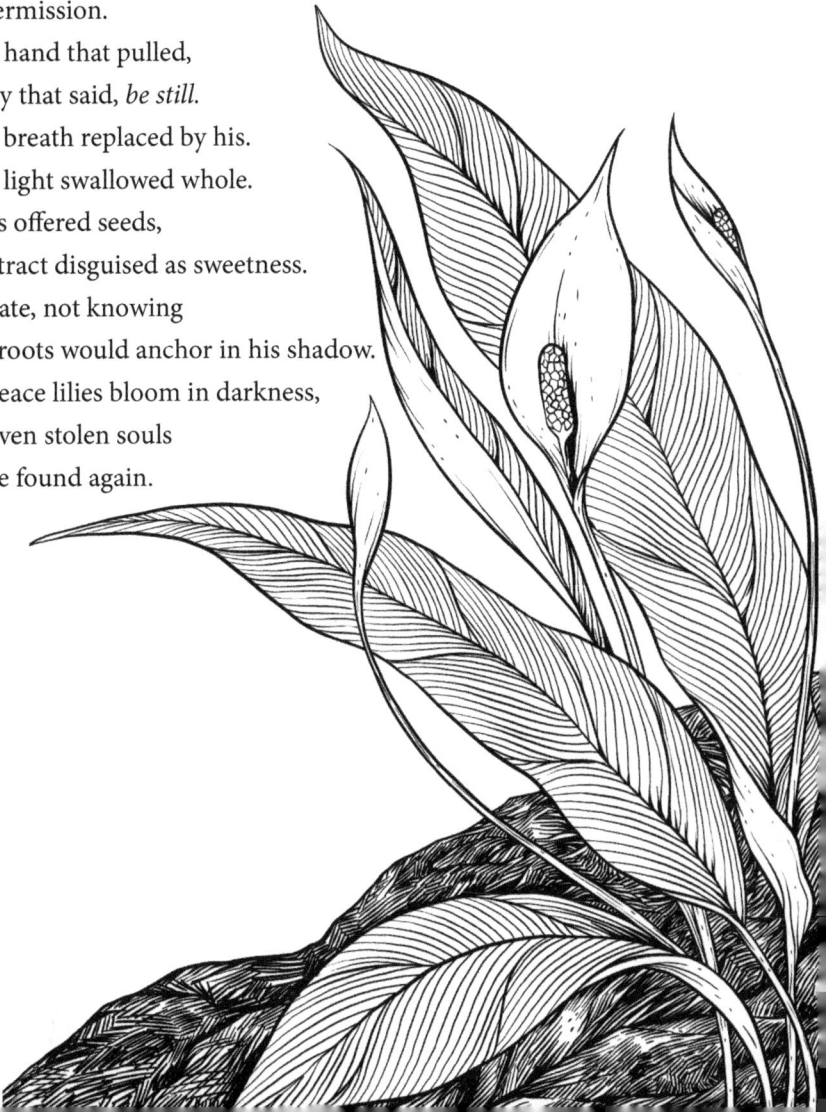

FOUR SEASONS OF RENEWAL

The husk collapses,
spilling seed into the hush—
a flicker beneath frost,
the whisper of roots dreaming in the dark.

What vanishes is never lost.
The river uncoils, the sky swallows itself whole,
and still, we search for endings
in the shape of the wind.

A HEART

One sliver away from broken—
the memory of us now unspoken.
You left my body
in deafening silence,
my mind lives in
a dark and quiet place
and there's no trace
of anything,
fools and kings have left the ring
and even though it's over
this weight stays on my shoulders.

You came with soft words
and the eyes of a sage.
But beneath your practiced kindness
was a hunger I could not see,
sharp as a knife hidden in velvet.
I was eager to heal,
to trust,
to believe that love
could be kind.

You took that kindness,
wrung it out like wet cloth,
squeezed until there was nothing left
but the worn threads of trust frayed and thin,
and all for what?
To feed your own emptiness,

to drink from the well
of someone so much younger,
untouched by the cynicism
you wore like a crown.

You asked for forgiveness
and called it love,
and I believed you.

I didn't see the hollow in your eyes,
how they looked past me
and saw only what you needed—
a vessel to fill,
a child to bend.

And when you were done,
you left my body in silence,
an empty room with no sound,
no trace of anything but loss.
Fools and kings have left the ring,
but the game was rigged from the start,
and even though it's over,
I'll hold this on my shoulders,
metamorphosing into a new world.

There's a quiet in me now,
a silence that remembers
the sting of your hands,
the way you turned sweetness
into something sharp,
used tenderness like a weapon.

And here I am,
trying to piece together
what you left in fragments,
trying to understand
how love became a debt
I never meant to owe.

WHEN A NARCISIST AND EMPATH MEET

it is an explosion of love
then . . . eggshells

more like shards of glass
wondering why the lump in your throat is growing. throbbing.
making words come out just regurgitates the glass you ate speaking
becomes too painful, too risky
like some wrong word will just rip your chords to shreds

AM I THE STORM

Pondering in a pool of muddied self-woe, am I the narcissist or the empath?
A constant self-interrogation, the kind that leaves your eyes bloodshot and blurry,
unable to see anything clearly, as if staring into cracked mirrors and searching for a whole reflection.

I sift through the silt of my own thoughts, dragging my fingers through the sludge of doubt,
feeling the weight of every memory that clings like hardened clay to my bones.
Did I take too much? Or did I give until I was hollow?
The lines are smeared, drawn in water that reflects back nothing but a distorted self.

There's a voice that whispers—
soft yet relentless—
in the back of my mind:
"Look closer, dig deeper."
So I dig with trembling hands,
but the more I search,
the more the mud thickens around me,
sticking like accusations I can't wash off.

I recount every conversation,
every moment I reached out,
wondering if it was to give or to grasp.
Did I pull them close to see them whole
or just to see myself reflected in their eyes?

Is my kindness a currency
I trade for affection?
Is my empathy a disguise
for the hunger I hide?

I wish for clarity,
but the pool only darkens
the deeper I go,
and the questions float like shadows
just beneath the surface.
I want to believe in my own tenderness,
but the doubt weighs heavy,
like stones in my pockets.

I am lost in this murky water,
swimming through my own intentions,
wondering if I am both the mirror and the fog—
both the hand that reaches
and the fist that pulls away.
Caught between the roles
of healer and harmer,
I wonder if I am the wound
or the one who caused it.

And still, I search—
through blurred vision,
through aching eyes—
for the truth that might redeem
or condemn me.
Am I the storm,
or just the cloud that carries it?

The line is so fine,
and I am treading it,
uncertain if I am drowning
or simply learning how to breathe.

SUN

He told me most girls get it done by a random guy in a gas station
he was doing me a favor
a gift that years later i call dissociation derealization
a permanent vacation that you can't escape from and there's no
sun . . .

> no sun
>
> no sun
>
> no sun
>
> no sun

so when I finally arched my back

and the bubble popped and my body cracked

> i drowned out all the ocean
> not a drop left of emotion now it's
> dissociation
> derealization
> a permanent vacation
> that you can't escape from and
> there's no sun

> no sun
>
> no sun
>
> no sun
>
> no sun

malleable with a mind of clay
when I buried me
gave my power away now I
dig in search of   water to
remind me I'm a daughter

so that his gas station.

incarceration.
and my derealization.
I can escape from
I'll find the sun

ISN'T IT ALWAYS LIKE THIS?

Hands that hold love like a loaded gun,
aimed at the ones who try to get close,
at the reflection that stares back too honestly,
at the parts of myself
that crave destruction over tenderness.

I see the mess I made,
like shattered glass across the floor,
and I step through it barefoot,
knowing I could have turned away,
knowing I chose this dance with pain.
I bleed and call it penance,
I ache and call it the cost of love.

Maybe I wanted the hurt,
the sharpness to remind me I'm alive—
a twisted kind of proof,
a way to feel in control
when the chaos within
spins too wildly to be named.

I play this game,
sabotage and sacrifice,
break what I build
just to have something to fix—
to feel needed,
to be the villain and the victim
all at once.

And here I am again,
staring at the damage,
heart clenched like a fist,
wondering if this time I've gone too far.
If this time, the bullet
won't just leave a scar,
but an empty space
where I used to be whole.

STRANGER

it is a *strange* thing. . . to hear

      understand

            learn

the one you loved never existed.

TEENAGE DREAMS

I feel as if I've lived the lives of many other souls, carrying their
memories, and fears of growing old— leaving cracks, open wounds
where all my love is sold. Manipulate the give and take, until I'm
forced to fold.

I'm lost inside a cloud, searching for land,
or maybe I'm too young to understand.

Teenage dreams, for those who feed off the naïve,
locked in chains, thinking we're free but they own the game.
In cloudy youth, can't see the truth—I'm tired of being used.

You told me that you're sorry for planting the seed,
but I can't stop it from growing inside of me.
Falling hard, clinging to my dignity—
years ago, they lost all their integrity.

I'm lost inside a cloud, searching for land,
or maybe I'm too young to understand

CONTROL

you may have one apple a day body. . .

        -head to heart

"SHE SEDUCED HIM"

Her eyes, dark with mischief,
became the flame that flickered
where whispers spread like wildfire
among the ever-watchful faces,
the judgmental grins
of those who'd never dared
to burn with such longing.

She was a charlatan, they said—
a girl too grown for her age.
They turned her into a cautionary tale,
the way they always do
with those who refuse to fold
into the quiet shapes of expectation.

In their eyes, she was a thief
a villain in the scripts they wrote,
but they didn't see how he
pursued her shadow,
the way he'd linger
in her presence,
as if the air around her
held the promise of a life
that could baptize.

They called her a seductress,
as if it were her hands
that pulled him in,
as if she wielded some power
other than the fire
of a young girl's hunger
for something beyond the dull ache
of coming of age.

They never knew how her nights ended
when the laughter died down—
sneers and cold shoulders,
branding her

They painted her in dark hues,
but they never saw the softness
of her heart, how it bled
when she was alone,
a canvas delicate
with desire.
She was a storm contained,
an ocean in a glass,
and they called her deceitful
because they couldn't see
past the ripples of her surface.

Behind closed doors, she wept,
wondered why the world
turned its back on her—
a girl who only knew how to love
with her whole being,

and in doing so,
became the target of
their tightly wound narratives
that left no room
for anything but fantasy.

They called her a liar
as she tried to
reclaim her purity.

WHAT KIND OF LOVE IS THIS—

opened me, sealed with your kiss,
blurry now—bit me,
a snake; I hear his rattle shake.

Intoxicated with poison,
didn't know how good venom tastes,
especially when it's wrapped
around your waist.

You say this love would last,
but I saw a snake in the grass—
you say this love is pure,
and how I'm just insecure.

Your words slither like shadows,
curl around my trust,
a hiss disguised as sweetness,
a bite I mistook for lust.

And now, as the venom spreads,
I feel your grip grow tight,
pulling me deeper into
the darkness of your night.

What kind of love is this—
that sinks its fangs so deep,
where poison feels like comfort
and lies rock me to sleep?

WABI SABI

I had not known darkness like this,

thick as ink and cold as iron,
a weight that presses the breath
from your lungs, makes the stars
above seem like pinpricks in the abyss.
And just like love,
the first time hurts the worst,
piercing and unexpected,
a knife slid between the ribs of reason.

A broken heart mends with time,
its fractures slowly fusing
with the soft glue of memory,
until it beats again in rhythm
with the world's indifferent pulse.
But darkness,
darkness is a different beast.
It clings like wet wool to the skin,
it seeps into the marrow,
and one must shake it off
with years of persistent, violent jolts—
each one a desperate bid for light,
each one a prayer to a god
you're trying to find

I learned to carry this shadow
like a reluctant companion,
one that crouches low behind me
when the sun is high
but stretches tall and monstrous
in the half-light of dusk.
It whispers in a voice that is my own,
of failures and fears,
of all the ways I could unravel
if I dared to let go
of its hand, even for a moment.

And yet, in those rare, trembling moments,
when I stumble upon a sliver of light
between the leaves of an old oak,
or in the gleam of a stranger's kind eyes,
I feel the darkness tremble.
For a second, it loosens its grip,
like a jealous lover sensing
the pull of a new desire.
And in that fleeting reprieve,
I remember what it is
to feel warm,
to feel whole,
to feel something other
than the heavy hum of survival.

But it is a fleeting thing—
this light, this hope—
slipping through my fingers
like water from a cupped hand.
And so, I return to the struggle,
to the violent jolts that rattle
the darkness loose,
bit by bit, piece by piece,
until the shape of it changes,
becomes something smaller,
something less consuming,
a shadow I can live with
rather than the monster
that devours me whole.

I search for the softness
in this hard-edged night,
for the lessons hidden in its folds—
that even the deepest dark
can't swallow you whole
if you keep moving,
keep reaching,
keep shaking off its weight
with a stubborn insistence
that there is still more to be seen,
still more to be felt,
still more to be lived.

And I know one day,
perhaps in the last moment of a long,
battered breath,
the darkness will loosen its hold
for good,
and I'll see the light,
not as a sliver or a glimpse,
but as the full, radiant bloom
it was always meant to be.
And in that moment,
I will know that I was never truly lost—
just wandering,
just learning,
just trying to find my way back
inside my heart.

MY RAGE TURNED ITS GAZE

The FBI called—
their words like cold metal on my skin,
telling me how you had done this before and will again.

If I don't tell them
each syllable a pinprick,
a puncture in my belief.
How you had whispered the same lies,
brushed the same hair behind an ear,
pulled her close with that same
gentle smile, and exclaimed
"you were written in the stars".

My blood ran cold
as if ice had settled in my veins,
a shiver curling through my bones
like smoke finding every hollow space.

In an instant, my whole vision changed—
the world cracked open,
each color I thought I knew
bled into something sharp, something jagged,
a shade that burned and twisted like rust.
Each shape remolded itself
into barbed wire and broken glass,
the familiar became foreign—
each memory now a splinter
underneath my skin.

You, a stranger to me,
your face a mask I had learned too well,
your voice a melody I had mistaken
for comfort, for warmth.
Not a friend to woman,
a shadow creeping through gardens,
stealing blooms and leaving thorns.

I see you now for what you are—
a wolf that wore a skin of love,
prowling in daylight with a softness
that hid the hunger in your eyes.
A devourer of trust,
a collector of hearts
you never planned to keep.

But in the wake of this knowledge,
something ignited deep within,
a rage I'd never known, a fire
that scorched my bones,
a blaze that consumed the spaces
where I had once stored tenderness.
I wanted to scream, to claw at the world
that allowed you to wander so freely,
to leave scars in your wake.

But I realized as the fire grew,
as it danced in the corners of my mind,
that it wasn't truly you—
not you, but the sickness inside you
that gnawed at your core.

You were not the beast, but the host,
not the villain, but the vessel.
A vessel spilling over with darkness,
with a poison that seeped
into the cracks of those you touched.

And so, my rage turned its gaze
not to the man, but to the shadows
that twist and writhe within him,
to the sickness that steals
the light from your eyes,
the illness that turns love
into something that devours,
something that stains.
I let my fury smolder,
not in vengeance, but in understanding—
that some are not born cruel,
but carry a sickness like a flame,
a sickness that burns all it touches,
until there is nothing left
but ash.

EVIL

Evil wants what it wants until you stop or kill it.

perhaps you thought it couldn't be stopped

SOLD MY SOUL

Then, it was something I forgot.
You came into view.
Because of me, you followed through.
They always ask if I'd like some ketamine,
But I know I need to find more of my mean.
I'm already Olympic level—
Twenty-four with eight gold medals.
I can dissociate,
drugs cannot replace.

I found this pain was fully mine.
I could beat it if I tried.
I found some clubs and ventured into the snow
of that December,
of when we said forever.
And in my head, I killed him again.

I sold my soul,
Sold my soul.
I didn't even know.

INHERITED DOMINION

There is a thread, a whisper of ancient blood,
an echo through the corridors of time, a vibrant strain that weaves
through history's seams—
older than kings, older than sin, older than the stones that build
empires on the backs of the broken.

Epstein, Trump—two names in a lineage, their ears attuned to the
somber murmur
of a voice that asserts, *this land is yours, and all it holds—its breath,
its bones, its bodies and their toil, its women, and its children*—all
for you, all *yours by birthright.*

This old poison seeps through eons, slithering through centuries
of conquest and crown,
a serpent's whisper in the ears of the puissant, hissing that they are
chosen, that the world
was forged to serve them and cower at their feet.

It proclaims this as divine mandate, etched in stars and bloodlines,
that any deviation is an affront to nature. Those who dare defy this
ordained decree,
those who resist, must be subdued, bent to fit the mold, or buried
beneath the weight of a sovereign boot.

In their private chambers, their gilded towers, their eyes gleam
with the secret knowledge
of an age-old fallacy: that wealth equals wisdom, that possession
confers power,
that dominion over flesh and earth is not theft but an inheritance.

And so, they gather in back rooms and hidden alcoves,
constructing altars from the remnants of the forsaken, while the strain persists,
a whisper that they, the chosen few, are the final and rightful arbiters of the world, that all who oppose are mere shadows to be silenced or shaped to fit their will.

Yet there is another strain rising, a new chorus of defiance, those who see through the veneer of deceit, who have lived beneath its crushing weight, and in their breath emerges a fresh song—
one that drowns out the ancient whisper, one that shatters the crowns of old rulers, and dismantles every stolen throne.

In the air lingers this new breath, a clarion call to those who know

LOVE OR CONTROL

You want me to wear you
like the clothes my mother bought me—
when I was brand new and scared too.

You want me to see you
like I've never been hurt.
But, darling, I want to, love you.

I'm haunted by something I don't know.
You call it love—
it feels more like control.
I need to be free. I need to know,
Do you love me,
or is it only control?

Can you see me,
past your reflection,
beyond our bodies?
Really know me?

How can you love me
if you won't let me grow?

I know it feels scary,
but you must let me go.
Maybe we'll meet
when we've both grown—
Be in the space we've always known.

Darling, I need to know:
Do you love me,
or is it only control?

I am a flower—
give me water and sun,
or let me go.

III. WAKING UP

In the light

A BEACON

All of that pain, let it wash away.
As I hold you, I'll keep the fear at bay.
Head above the water, won't let you slip under,
I know the current's strong—
but, darling, I am stronger.

Come to me, bruised and heavy-laden,
shadows of battles fought in silent corners,
where hands once took without asking,
where the cost of survival was silence.

Yet here, in the sanctum of this embrace,
we strive to soften the edges,
to cleanse wounds that were never ours to carry,
to reclaim the names stolen from our tongues.

Let the waves of sorrow dissolve beneath our touch,
for I am your steadfast anchor in this rolling sea,
resolute and unyielding,
stronger than the tide that tried to pull us under.

Nobody knows the quiet struggles we shoulder,
the hidden tears, the broken dreams.
But in this moment, let us release the weight of the world,
as we grow new eyes that see.

With every breath, reclaim what was taken,
inch by inch, rebuild and heal.

Darling, we are stronger—together, unbroken,
a beacon against the shadows that once made us small.
I'm sorry I left you, to be claimed by those you did not belong to.
You are not 'for' them, though they believed you are.

As I've gotten older, my stomach for abuse has gotten weaker.
I can no longer be for you.
The more you say "I am"
the less you are
for in this fleshy car
is something as old as a far off star
Yoga means to unite
This is a union, not a fight
I can no longer be for you,
I am the less you are.

LIVING INSIDE

and one day you just see
      when the veil starts to lift
          and the cloud's less thick
             living inside

SHADOW

I sought refuge in the gentle underbelly of "victim,"

a haven where the label's warmth
offered escape from self-revelation,
a space to hide from the glaring truth
of my own potent, shadowed self.

They say women are carved from sorrow,
their souls shaped by the weight of suffering,
while men, with pain on the outside
are drawn to these unspoken wounds.

I longed to shed the confines of "victim,"
to rise from its embrace and find solace
in a new identity.

NOW I KNOW THAT I KNOW.

HEALING

In sterile rooms, where hope once lingered,
Through eye movements, meticulously traced,
I pursued the fragments of my past,
Yet the healing remained elusive, distant.

The protocols, the sessions,
Failed to touch the depth of my wound,
A heart scarred, a spirit fragmented,
In the shadows of silence, pain endured.

But in the forest's embrace,
Where the air is drenched in life,
I rediscovered the echoes of my being,
In the quiet presence of trees and earth.

The leaves rustled with a soothing cadence,
The soft touch of the breeze a gentle reminder,
Unveiling the self long buried,
In nature's quiet, I saw the reflection of my own spirit.

No longer ensnared by clinical confines,
I found clarity in the natural world,
A mirror of authenticity,
Revealing the self I had almost forgotten.

PLATOS TWO WORLD THEORY

There is only the construct of man and the universe.
EMDR was not enough—it is beyond, the soul resides.

MY OWN VOICE

And with the sound of my own voice—something stretched deep within my belly,

A snake coiling up my throat, singing.

There was the sound of my own voice,

An "I am" swollen under my tongue, finally released.

And with the sound of my own voice, I heard the first echo,

A wabi-sabi cry that shattered my heart and ripped through my vocal cords.

This great sound bounced off the walls of my world, and suddenly direction became clearer,

For I felt the reverberation of truth—

Both mine, and yours, and ours.

ROOTED

for a woman
safety is learned

like a tree
moved from cement to soil
roots sinking, branches reaching—
as she was always meant to.

but in this world
unsafety was familiar
and safety a privilege
too distant to trust

yet in her sisters' hands
in mother earth's embrace
she remembers—
she was never meant to fear
she was always meant to grow.

and together
they fertilize the earth
turning pain into rich soil
so the next can rise stronger.

for courage is the deepest root
and the best protection of all.

IN THE CRADLE OF THE FORESTS ARMS

Where sunlight weaves through ancient boughs,
I wandered lost, yet found again,
In nature's deep and timeless vows.

The whispering leaves called out my name,
Their murmur soft as summer rain,
And with each step upon the earth,
I felt the pulse of life regain.

Among the ferns and mossy stones,
I saw the remnants of my soul,
Fragments scattered, long forgotten,
Now rising, yearning to be whole.

The scent of pine, the touch of wind,
Reawakened parts of who I'd been,
Saying soft "remember me"
In nature's breath, I found my kin.

The flowers showed their tender grace,
With petals bruised yet still embraced,
They bore the storm, the wind's fierce gale,
Yet from their wounds, new blooms set sail.

The oak tree stood in stoic might,
Its branches reaching for the sky,
It whispered calm in my embrace,
To observe, to breathe, to give my weight.

"Endure," it said, "through trials wear,
In stillness find your healing there.
For only through deep awareness found,
Can one's true self be unbound."

In the trees and murmuring streams,
I glimpsed the fragments of lost dreams,
The echoes of a spirit strong,
In every rustling leaf and song.

Here, in the cradle of the wild,
I found my essence, pure and mild,
A spirit rekindled, once again,
In nature's arms, where I begin.

The remnants of my soul emerged,
From shadows deep and wounds submerged,
And in this place, so vast and free,
I birthed new eyes that could see.

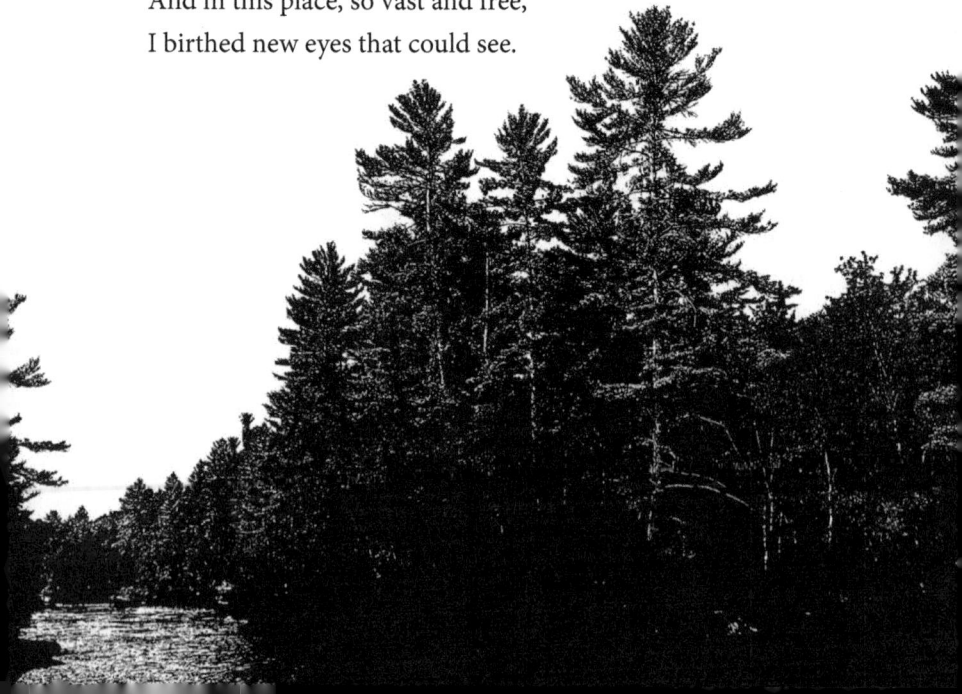

EROTIC SELF

Perhaps the erotic self that was taken,
A fragment borrowed, never truly mine,
Was a sacred right, a divine passage—
A journey through this life,
To claim and hold,
A whispered truth of existence.

PUSSY PAPAYA

Sweet nectar
Flows from the river
Fruit of the vine
A woman's divine
Pussy papaya
It's all inside yah
So deep and full
Powerful
Impossible to fathom
The push and pull in tandem
Delicious and pure
All that is her
Pussy, pussy papaya
From near and far
The power's inside yah
Pussy papaya
Pussy, pussy papaya
The power inside
Sweet woman divine
All of the muses
Come from these juices
Flowing inside yah
Pussy papaya
She walks in power
Creation inside her
Nature's cure
Of death and rebirth
Don't try to make sense

Entity goddess
All that she is
Is all that there is
Give thanks to the mamas
Pussy papaya
From near and far
The power's inside yah
Pussy papaya
Pussy, pussy papaya
The power inside
Sweet woman divine

WE ARE MEANT TO DWELL IN THIS BODY

I once contemplated the final dusk
Perched upon that solitary hill,
A precipice where the world's edges met
And whispered of endings.

In that silent solitude, the wind carried an echo
Of a profound and unsettling truth—
An urge to leave this life behind,
As if I had already exhausted its promises.

I envisioned the leap, the release,
A transition into what lay beyond
This worn existence,
A desire born of weariness and despair.

Yet in that hushed space of contemplation,
I unearthed a deeper revelation—
The call I felt was not an invitation
To surrender my life, but to embrace transformation.

The ache I harbored was not for departure
But for the shedding of the self I had outgrown,
The ancient skin of my past existence,
The serpent coiled along my spine, heavy with history.

This skin, an old garment of memories and mistakes,
Must lie dormant and still,
Until the final, trembling moment of release,
When I could cast off the layers that once bound me.

The transition is not an escape
But a profound metamorphosis—
A chance to break free from the shackles of yesterday,
From the clandestine fates that awaited me in shadows.

We are bound to this vessel of flesh,
Not to abandon it but to evolve within its confines,
To stretch, to grow, and to renew
In the crucible of our own becoming.

We are meant to dwell in this body,
To embrace its trials and tribulations,
To molt and to bury the old skin
Deep within the earth's nurturing embrace.

In this process of transformation,
I discovered a new understanding—
That the journey of life is not about escape,
But about embracing change and finding rebirth
In the cycles of our own creation.

And so, I remain,
Bound to this existence,
Not by chains, but by the possibility of growth,
To bury the past and rise anew,
Ever evolving in the tapestry of life.

CHOICE

I choose not to hate,

a sickness hidden
in a shadowed cell,
beyond the light's reach.
It festers in silence,
an unseen blight.
I embrace the space
where light and clarity dwell,
letting them dissolve
the darkness within.

I AM AN INFINATE BEING

This truth, a mantra etched in the core of our existence,
Becomes a refuge when shadows creep in,
Twisting and coiling around my fragile essence,
A dark mist that seeks to obscure light.
Yet, I remember:
I am an infinite being.

In moments when darkness presses heavy,
This light force within me expands,
A brilliance that stretches beyond my physical form,
Filling spaces within and without.
My spirit swells to encompass the vast expanse,
A luminous force that stretches further,
Pushing back against encroaching gloom.

Shadow, relentless and consuming,
Can only serve light,
For it is in presence of darkness
That this inner brilliance shines most fiercely.
Becoming larger than the boundaries of my skin,
A vessel in which light and shadow intermingle.

Shadow, though fierce and unyielding,
Is transient, destined to ebb and recede,
Leaving behind trails of lessons and revelations.
It is through this interplay of dark and light
That I come to understand the breadth of my being.

As darkness retreats,
It leaves a quiet resonance,
A reminder of infinite space within,
Where light and shadow converge.
And in this vast, unending realm,
I find my true self.

IT HAS TO COME FROM YOU

I wept and called for help, always alone in these moments—

> Why?
> Because I isolate myself there.

> She came over, placing her hand on my womb,
> A touch gentle, an offering of solace.

> Feel to heal,
> Feel to heal,

> Breathe.

> It has to come from you.

NATURES NURTURING

Phytoncides that ride frequencies unseen—breathe them in,
Light and sin, nature is there,
she's hyper-prepared so just be self-aware.

There is no such thing as good and bad,
but shadow and light—
the moon and the night,
the spheres we ebb and flow,
dancing toe to toe with the shadow,
and you can handle anything,
just breathe and be in your body.

Advance with the spirit of boundless possibilities,
You are infinite—an eternal being,
A spirit in the vessel of human experience.
Embrace the spectrum of feeling, and the journey of healing.

You are magic—a witchy child,
Expanding through every crevice,
Breathing through the coils so tightly bound,
and that is where the trauma is found,
the stuck energies preventing you to see.
You are love, you are loved, you are the universe.

In nature's touch, find the balm for the soul.
Phytoncides, those elusive compounds in forest air,
Are known to enhance immune function and reduce stress,
Their subtle frequencies attuning to your deepest needs.

The rustle of leaves and the whisper of the trees,
Calm the inner storm and bring tranquility.
Sunlit meadows and ancient groves,
Infuse vitality where it once was lost,
Allowing the earth's restorative energy to flow through you.

Talk to the trees,
as Hesse said they are "penetrating preachers",
if you know how to see.

IDENTITY IS JUST A TRANSIENT STORY

Nature's all there is.
Identity is just a transient story;
Nature is all there is.

The more we sever ourselves,
The more we harm.
The more we sever ourselves,
The more we harm.
Identity is all in our minds;
We've gone blind.

Nature, call to nature.
Never thought that I could be
Sitting here with you—
Something from beyond,
Something in a song.

ALL THAT WAS

Monsters under the bed
Flew out of her head
When she saw the shadows in you.
Through the streets, she roamed,
Doing things that can't be told,
Till she found the shadows in her.

They said, "I'm gonna eat you whole,
With a heart as pure as gold,
And a soul as deep as the ocean."

But with this beast, she fell in love
And saw that nothing was as it seemed
Or as she dreamed of.
She fell in love
With all that was.

IV'E ALWAYS SAID

I wanted to be a 'real person'—
Pinocchio
something so deeply flesh,
it was more like stars.

So human, I would feel all,
uncrafted by the world,
safe from fantasy,
my mind as my own,
a 'real' girl.

ENERGY CANNOT BE CREATED OR DESTROYED

I saw them—
Corpses laid out empty,
Of what had once fulfilled them.

I saw them—
Each was a wish to die,
A peaceful confession of transience.
And yet none
It only transformed itself,
Born again.

I saw all
Twisted in one,
Moon and sun,
Shapeshifter.

I saw them—
Faces of who I've been,
Faces that housed the familiar,
Broken men and women,
And all in between.
Strange beasts.

and in the jungle, before reading Hesse
I saw them—
a carp, its mouth opened in ache,
the dying shimmer of its silver eye

turning toward something I could not name.
I saw a child,
red with the heat of new breath,
its cry folding into the folds of time.
I saw hands
gripping the soft hilt of harm—
a blade—
and in that same breath,
the wrists bound,
the body bent before the blade returned.
Bodies—
naked, interlaced, trembling—
moaned into flame,
then laid flat, cooled by silence,
all motion undone.
I saw the heads of creatures:
boars, crocodiles, bulls, birds,
their eyes bright with origin.
And I saw the gods,
not separate from the beasts,
but part of their breathing—
rising, breaking,
folding into each other
in a thousand invisible threads.
They were not dying.
They were shifting—
each shape a gate,
each face a turning.
They wore new masks
before the old ones faded.
All of it flowed—

rested—
breathed and broke again.
One body of many names,
glimpsed beneath a skin
like riverlight.
I touched it—
that trembling surface—
and it was my face.
And my face was smiling.
A smile
not of joy or sorrow,
but of knowing.
A smile that held
both the rising and the falling,
the wound and the healing,
and everything in between.
And this,
perhaps,
is how the wise ones smile—
when they finally
stop trying to escape what already is.

MUSIC

Let music cradle the soul, unburden the body,
reaching toward heaven and hell more than words ever could,
telling your story more than words ever should.

FREE

Running through my memory

Trouble watch over me

Silent still, steals the sound

Bury me, underground

Falling down with the leaves

Spruce, pine and evergreen

I feel the moss, breathe the sky

Catch a briar, scrape my eye

Do you remember me?

Do you remember me?

Now I am free

Clean myself off with the earth

Clean away all of the hurt

Clean myself off with the earth

Clean Away

Clean Away

Clean Away

IN WHOSE EYES

In whose eyes, I feel myself unravel
Bird of my soul, a hundred towers I have known
Fortified lie, but now in your eyes. . .

Feels like flowers growing inside
a return to wild
Feels like power, flowing through life
a return to nature

In your eyes, I feel past my body
Maybe it is love, but it feels like a awakening

Feels like fire, burning inside
a return to wild
Feels like power, flowing through life
a return to nature

grow, know, in whose eyes?

In whose eyes I feel
myself unravel?

in whose eyes. . .

A RETURN TO WILD

I no longer am for you
Perfected by the insatiable hunger of being wanted,
Valuing my reflection only through the prism
of your predatory eyes.
This endless adulation—
A commerce of craving pulling at the threads of my soul,
Broadcast by tiny screens in our pockets,
And billboards that loom like false gods in the sky.

An inescapable patriarchy shaped my mind
To desire harm, to long for visibility,
Not for my powerful softness,
Not for the ancient wisdom I carry,
But for the tightness of my clothes,
The fleeting spark of youth in my eyes.

I want to be as wild as my observer:
The butterfly, transformed in the shadows,
Emerging anew in her quiet defiance.
The trees, who give freely to man—
Even as we use and abuse their grace.
The animals, who love us as friends,
Yet remind us daily of our harm and their consent

Within the eye of the wild, I am all she is:
This beautiful earth—growing, giving, alive and free.

THE KINDNESS OF PAIN

Although we have walked through the underworld and lingered in the in-between—where fog blurs the lines of clarity—we now see the light, its brilliance magnified by the shadows we have known. We hear the birds with piercing sweetness, their songs sharper because there was a time when we could not hear. We feel our hearts more tenderly, their beats an intimate rhythm, deliberate, because once, we could not feel.

When we stretch our conscious minds, we begin to see the pomegranate seeds—the very ties that once bound us to darkness—not as shackles, but as gifts. In Greek mythology, Persephone's consumption of the pomegranate tethered her to the underworld, binding her to its cycles of loss and return. Yet, from this act emerged transformation. What was once a symbol of confinement becomes a key to profound wisdom—wisdom forged through pain, through cycles, through the delicate balance between descent and ascent.

I believe the kindest people are those who have known the kindness of pain—who would never inflict suffering on another for their own gain. This deep understanding of darkness carries a sacred duty: to teach, to protect, and to transmute shadow into light. Knowing the difference between boundaries and demands.

This is the kindness of pain: it teaches, it deepens, it reveals. The seeds of the underworld remain the same, but the lens through which we see them shifts—they can become offerings, reminders that even in darkness, there is something to harvest. By embracing both realms, we gain the strength to honor the night while rising to the dawn, carrying with us the gifts of our journey.

Together, we build another world—a world woven from resilience, forged in shadows, and illuminated by the light we once doubted we would ever see again. In this world, we honor what we have endured, and in that honoring, we create something new: a place where pain and joy coexist, where wisdom is shared, where we are made whole—not in spite of our scars, but because of them.

www.ingramcontent.com/pod-product-compliance
Lightning Source LLC
Chambersburg PA
CBHW052106090426
42741CB00009B/1691